Driver of Wealth

All the tools you will need to win as a delivery driver.

By: Jack Robert Masden

For my loving wife,

Martha, and my son

John

-J.R.Masden

Contents

[Tables](#)

[Preface](#)

[Introduction](#)

[1: Routine](#)

[2: Be Humble](#)

3: Tools you will need

4: Apply what you have learned

5: Ideal Vehicle

6: Automate your Life

7: In and Out

8: Define your Wealth

9: Acknowledgements

10. Citations

PREFACE

Just a few years ago I found myself at odds working a job that I was content on leaving however, it did not take long for me to realize that the job I had was to easy to get ahead financially. It was the "diamond in the rough". I have made many friends that have graduated from colleges with high honors and a crisp Diploma to back it up with, for them I tip my hat off and say a job well done. It was not long until the cheering ended when they came to realize that for many of them their Student loan payments were about to take effect. I fortunately steered clear and did everything in my power to achieve financial independence making less than $40,000 dollars a year annually as a "Delivery Driver".

If you are looking to become the best delivery driver, you're in luck! Within this book I have compiled a list of sure-fire methods to increase your tips, time management skills, and overall Expert knowledge in becoming the best delivery driver.

Have you ever stopped and thought geez what do I need to do to increase my tips I'm just not making as much as I should be?

there must be a better way? Whether you are starting off as a brand-new delivery driver unsure about how to interact with your very first customer. I will help you through the process ahead and give you the kickstart to thrive in the fast-paced work environment among your peers. For all the seasoned delivery drivers out there, I have also included ideas and strategies you can add to take yourself to the next level and possibly become the top performing employee of the year.

Do not settle for average push yourself, because no one is going to do it for you remember this you control your financial future take action, generate waves of income, and live the life you deserve become the Driver of Wealth.

Let's dive right in shall we:

Chapter 1

Routine

Everyone at some point in their lifetime has traded time for money and if you picked this book up chances are you have overheard a lot of people say how that's the worst thing anyone can do. Well I say in our line of work we don't have that luxury. Here's your first tip from me to you: "Build a routine" Routines can be an anchor. No matter what's going on in our day, knowing that we will be having our evening meal around 6 pm, and going to bed around 10 pm, can be a real comfort. The certainty of our routine can help us to manage the uncertainty that life can throw up. Coping with unpredictable periods of time can feel more doable when we have a little structure in place to look to. Having a daily routine can help to reduce our stress levels. Trying to remember things can be really stressful and can fill our brains up with everything on our 'to do' list; which can be incredibly overwhelming. When we have a routine, a lot of the things we do day-to-day turns into muscle memory, and we don't have to think about them anymore. Routine can take the guesswork and uncertainty out of bits of our day, which can allow us to feel more in control and less stressed. Having a routine can help us to cultivate positive daily habits and to prioritize self-care. Organizing our time gives us the opportunity to build in blocks of time for things that are important to us. This can allow us to build in daily habits that help us with driving safer. It could include things like time to relax, or a regular bedtime. When they're part of our routine, it can make it easier to keep up with them because we have the time to do them and they become our 'new normal'. One of the things that having a regular routine can really help with, is sleep. Sleep is really important for our mental health because going to bed and waking up at a similar time most days allows our body to get used to our sleep-wake cycle and sets our sleep-wake clock accordingly. This means that by having a regular sleep routine, especially if we build in some time to wind down before we go to bed each day, we should begin to find that we find it easier to get to sleep and sleep better once we are asleep. Creating a routine allows us to build in time for the important things. This includes time to rest, relax, and have fun. It's not perfect – there are always going to be days when something overruns, a job takes three times as long as we expect it to take, or someone pops in unexpectedly. But structuring our time to include some downtime increases the likelihood that we'll manage to have that time most days. We will all value different things – for some of us it might be going to the movies.

For many of us, it will be something else entirely, but that's why our daily routines are individual to us. As a delivery driver time is everything to us, we must master how we walk, talk, and drive. They play a key factor when it comes to making money because getting to your destination can get tiring your ability to move quickly makes every bit of difference. Your physical health plays a special part when it comes to delivering, I won't tell you to diet but instead just try living a happier lifestyle try to think of building your strength more than trying to lose weight. Challenge to stick to a goal for at least a month whether its jogging or walking your pet an extra mile. When it comes to overall appearance, a well dressed delivery driver can give off the notion to the customer "Im here and I care".

A quick little story on this: when I was making a delivery to a customer that lived in a 3 story complex as I got to the door he swung the door open and said that was fast I saw you from the moment you pulled up looks like you broke a sweat trying to get up those stairs. Now I'm not out of shape it was just 99 degrees out that day, I replied back with yea its nothing I love what I do and just like that he pulls a 10 dollar bill out of his pocket and says here's for your hard work and dedication to duty sir.

In their head they get a perspective of how their food is being cared for it may seem kind of weird but you have to think of the food product as a prized possession because in essence that's what it eventually turns out to be once it leaves your hands to its rightful owner. If you are carrying the product carelessly and it's designed to be eaten a certain way i.e. "Pizza" you do not want to carry it upside down or shake it everywhere because the presentation also plays a key factor in repeat business and if you deliver a pile of marinara with a pepperoni on top chances are they are not calling to your business again and we will have missed out on an opportunity to create our wealth chain of repeat customers.

Chapter 2

Be Humble

According to Forbes magazine article the 13 Habits of Humble People in 2019 Studies have shown that humble people are more likely to help friends than their prideful counterparts.

As a result, they maintain stronger personal and professional relationships. A study of more than 1,000 people—with roughly 200 in leadership positions—revealed that companies with humble people in leadership positions had a more engaged workforce and less employee turnover. As a delivery driver that plays such a big factor when it comes to interacting with the customer. "Humility is the true key to success.

Even the most successful drivers lose their way at times. They often embrace and overindulge from the fruits of success. Humility halts this arrogance and self-indulging trap. Humble people share the credit and wealth, remaining focused and hungry to continue the journey of success". Some can relate to this situation there's nothing more annoying than being in a conversation with somebody who you can just tell is dying to get his or her words in. When you see their mental gears spinning, it's a sign they're not listening but rather waiting to speak. Why? Because they believe that what they have to say is more valuable than listening to you. In other words, they're placing their self-interest first. Don't interrupt the customer if they open the door and just start spouting about how great their day was instead give them more encouragement to give them the assurance you work for a company that cares.

"Don't be that FedEx driver who throws the package over the fence in the backyard and drives off". As hilarious it may seem to some that customer that received that package more than likely took a huge profit margin away from FedEx due to the viral video being posted. Now there's going to be a time when you are frustrated maybe from work or from something that happened before you arrived that day. Look whatever it is you got to do your best to let things go for the time being because if you want to create that path to wealth you don't want to be

Spartan Kicking a customer's door because maybe the customer before him did not leave you a tip. Trust me on this I have been delivering for years not to boast just my experience. To caveat off this notion of bewildered attitude if it's an experience that happened before you arrived to work or something that is pending post work either way you don't have control over the situation while delivering. So put that mess to the side always remember, what your working hard for say to yourself "I'm here to build WEALTH!"

Chapter 3

Tools You Will Need

Now we got to put some pep in that step baby were here to make "Money". To acquire the right pep, we need the proper shoes. I know what you might be thinking what's wrong with the running shoes I got on my feet relax boss I'm getting there. So typically, when people go out to run errands or hangout with friends you want to just throw your running shoes on and not look back that's ok for that aspect. However, when we hit the road for our delivery jobs that's not the most ideal way to go here's why. Running shoes were intended to keep you moving at a very rapid pace therefore the padding and area surrounding the top of your feet are hardly protected. As a delivery driver if you have been working long enough you have dropped something on your foot at least once or twice unfortunately. I have good news I have tried and tested the most optimal

performing go faster and their quite common some of you may be actually wearing a pair and they are drum roll please......
"Trail Runners",

Yes, I have found these to be the best when it comes to

overall durability and comfort for the long days ahead. For one they have padding in all the right spots, the structure of how your feet are kept in is my favorite part of all because with running shoes your feet tend to slide around when it gets wet outside and most don't do well during the rainy days which are the days we accumulate the best tips. Running shoes become easily saturated nobody wants to run around with wet feet with the trail runners on if I know the weathers going to be horrible ahead of time I spray a coat of rain protection over the top to keep my feet from getting drenched. Finally, is the traction for when you must go through grass and muddy areas. You can find a decent new pair for about $70 dollars don't worry you will make the difference back with your protected feet or you can find used for cheaper at a thrift store or Ross if you got one nearby and they last two times longer than your typical running shoes enough said go get you a pair what are you waiting for. Some other optional items I highly recommend you have with you while delivering are covered under these next four categories laid out by Courier Hacker.

Let's start in the place we all spend most of our time. Depending upon your driving situation, you want to make sure everything going on in the driver's seat is fluid and increases your safety while driving.

The first thing you're going to need is a phone mount. If you're still storing your phone in a cup holder while driving, it's time to step up your game.

There's a variety of mounts available that vary in size and grip, but I recommend you think about what will work for your workflow. If you prefer something that will make it easy to grab your phone and go, get one that has a magnetic mount.

　Alternatively, there are some good choices for making it easy to look over at your screen while driving. Some are made to attach to your windshield. If you have some dashboard space available next to your steering wheel, I recommend the one I own. It also has a quick release grip that is more secure than the magnet mount.

Keeping Charged

Using your phone constantly while on shift can kill your battery, especially if your phone isn't brand new. So, how do you make sure your phone doesn't die in the middle of a delivery?

The first thing you'll need is a charging cord. Most newer cars have a USB port that you can plug into conveniently. Depending on its location in the car, I recommend getting a length that will reduce cord clutter as much as possible. My port is in the front of my center console, so a 1.5-foot cord is perfect.

If you have an older car, don't fret. There are still plenty of options for charging your phone on the go. If you need a Bluetooth connector for your car, you can find one with USB ports for charging.

    Not delivering with a car? Do a lot of walking? Don't feel like charging in your car (for some reason)? Don't worry, I've got a couple of options for you. If you're into your phone being a brick, you can get a phone case that has a battery built into it. If you want to have a cord hanging out of your pocket, there's a great portable external battery from Anker.

Making Deliveries

Depending upon which company you drive for, the bags you receive to get you going may be different. The small bags you receive when getting started with GrubHub or Postmates are fine and great for single orders. But for GrubHub, at least, the big bag I received at first was no good. It's flimsy, awkward to carry, and I got rid of it immediately.

So what's a good alternative for big

orders? I've actually come up with a great set up.

First, you're going to want to grab a big that is sturdy and easy to carry. I found a commercial insulated food delivery bag on Amazon and it is perfect. It fits plenty of food (even most pizzas, although I recommend grabbing a separate pizza bag) and is almost as easy to carry as the small bags.

Still have more bags after filling this up? I've got you covered. Grab some food delivery boxes. They fit easily in a trunk alongside your bags, and they're great for separating orders or temperatures (one for hot, one for cold).

Finally, one of my biggest pet peeves is drinks. Sometimes, you get orders with more drinks than you can handle. You only have two hands, and your car only has so many cup holders. The solution is getting a couple additional portable cup holders. They're easily storable and getting two will make any huge drink order smooth.

Extra Gadgets

To round out your arsenal, there are a few extra goodies that will help make your workflow smoother.

If your car has keyless locks and trunk release, then a key lanyard can be a lifesaver. If you've got a huge order and need to set down bags just to get to your keys in your pocket, having this can make it super easy to click your unlock or trunk opener so you can set everything down.

If you're big on stacking orders, sticky notes are a must. These make it easy to put names on bags, drinks, boxes, and everything you need to separate.

If you're ever in a restaurant and bored, or if you get a call while carrying bags, think about investing in wireless earbuds. This is by far the most optional item on this list, but I got this wireless single earbud on Amazon and it's pretty nifty for discreetly watching YouTube videos while waiting a while at restaurants.

Chapter 4

Apply What you have learned

If you don't apply what you learn then learning loses most of its value. For example, suppose you learn that exercising makes you happier and increases your lifespan, both goals you greatly desire. If you don't exercise as a result of learning that, then it didn't do much good to you. Indeed, it might have made you feel stressed out, which in turn decreases your happiness and lifespan!

This is not to say that unapplied knowledge is always useless. For example, some people get intrinsic enjoyment out of learning. There is also the potential benefit of "working out" your mind and increasing its ability to learn things quickly.

On the whole, however, a huge proportion of the value of learning comes from applying what you've learned. Yet for some reason people are generally not great at that. I can teach you everything in this book, but it all means nothing unless you follow through with it. Ok now that you got your money makers on let's work on the speech part. Yes, anyone can go up to a door knock and give the greeting of the day that's what I classify as (Robo-Talk). Yea we need to not do that because we're here to make "Money!". First things first you need to work on your "Growth Mindset" in order to maximize those tips. There was a study done by Rescue Time: Blog that found people with a growth mindset believe abilities—like talent and intelligence—can be developed through dedication and hard work. They're more likely to enjoy learning, seek out situations to experiment, and see failure as an opportunity to grow.

Try to visualize yourself as a marketing "Machine" you want to attract the customer, so he/she has something to remember you by. A little example: On my way out of the military everyone is required to take a class that provides you the tools to find a job in the not so organized society we all live in. well on the 4th day of this two week transitioning class there was a speaker named Joe. Joe taught us all a very valuable lesson when he finished his spiel on how to create a well diverse Resume Joe asked the whole class a question. "What was the first thing you all thought about me when I walked in?" a friend of mine answered "That bright Pink shirt has got to go

GQ" of course we all laughed Joe answered back and said if you all don't take anything from the Resume lesson remember what that GQ jokester in the back room said "Ladies and Gentlemen first impressions are everything".

Building a catch phrase might not be a bad thing to try out, if you have ever stayed up way to late and watched the news you have those reporters that end there night with a self-proclaimed classic catch phrase like "That's all Folks!" to give the notion that they are done and are signing off. You should try to incorporate this method not the same exact words but your own for instance when the customer opens the door and your delivering food analyze the body language if they seem to be jubilant say "I'm on a twenty day diet, so far I have lost ten days". Or whatever gets the customer to laugh and open a bit. Laughing should at least increase that happy endorphin to push that tip number a little higher I mean let's be honest nobody likes to talk to a mannequin.

Chapter 5

Ideal Vehicle

Now that you have built up your arsenal of tip raising skills and are moving and communicating to the best of your ability it's time to Drive! I may hurt some feelings in this segment but in the end, you will thank me I will be saving you a boatload so you can really start growing your wealth pyramid. If you plan on driving anything but a compact car for delivering, it's going to take you longer to accumulate wealth. According to Your Mechanic news article in 2019 The "Toyota Corolla has long been known for its reliability", which is very important if you're going to get those pizzas delivered before they get cold. It's also easy on gas, and because the Corolla is so popular, you should have no difficulty in finding a used model at a reasonable price.

Although if you don't have much of a choice in the matter, I still want you to take this part in so in case you change your mind or find yourself a car later on down the road you can still use this segment. You must take in the price of fuel, labor on the vehicle, and if you're driving a big truck those tires will get expensive. An alternative method if you don't have the money or time to trade your vehicle in for the compact car you could always ask a friend or family member to possibly loan you theirs and give them a small kick back that way you alleviate the hassle of having to buy a new or used and you don't have to worry about the upkeep.

For the time being it is what it is you do the best with what you got. When it comes to delivering smaller compact cars win almost every time especially if your delivering in a densely populated area. Have you ever tried backing up a heavy duty extended crew cab near your county courthouse on a Monday if so, I feel your pain buddy? The ability to get in and out makes all the difference. I would also like to fill you in on a little info if your new to the whole delivery driving world nobody cares that you have to be somewhere at a certain time so when the time comes and it will squeezing through traffic jams in a car will cut time on the road which is what we want in a safe manner of course….(cough).

Chapter 6

Automate Your Life

The beauty behind simplistic automation; in my eyes Wealth cannot be created by one action but by a multitude of calculated decisions that are put in place to free your mind of the avoidable financial stressor' so you can put your focus on the day at hand.

In this chapter I'm going to help layout a

plan of action to get you on the right track. The key is to "set it and forget it" think about it, if you are not doing this yet almost all wealthy individuals will not be seen walking in to the water department in a three piece suit to pay a $95 dollar water bill its just not worth the time.

The current year is 2019 there are apps on your cell phone that can send you updates and confirmations on when your bills are due or paid it's too easy people make it happen. Step three once you establish how much you have left over from paying your monthly necessities take the difference and split it up into four different categories' these are Fuel, Vehicle

Maintenance, Savings, and Investing. After completing all these steps in this chapter give your planning a solid month and make sure your budget is working the way it's supposed to. If by then everything's moving smoothly pat yourself on the back, you are already doing better than most delivery drivers.

Money is a leading cause of stress for the majority of Americans, according to the American Psychological

Association. One big reason money is so stressful is because some people grapple with making choices about money all the time. Many Americans are constantly deciding what bills to pay, how much to save, and how much to spend.

But, what if there was an easier way? What if you could put your money on autopilot and then just sit back and let your cash work for you? The good news is, you probably can if you just automate your financial life. How to automate your finances putting your finances on autopilot is simple and it makes it much easier to do the right things with your money. The process starts with taking a close look at your budget and deciding how much you want to save and how much you want to spend.

Once you've decided on your savings rate, set up automatic contributions to different savings accounts. You should set up automatic contributions to:

A retirement savings account: This could be a workplace 401(k) or an IRA. Ideally, you'll want to contribute at least 15% of your income to your retirement fund -- although this can include 401(k) matching funds from your employer.

An emergency fund: If you don't have an emergency fund covering three to six months of living expenses, saving one should be your first priority after taking care of retirement.

A college account: If you have kids, contribute to a 529 and get tax breaks to save for education. Savings account for other goals: This could be an account to fund purchasing a home, a new car, travel, new furniture, or whatever you want to spend money on.

The specific amount to save will vary

depending upon your goals. If you plan to buy a house in five years and need a $30,000 down payment, set up automatic contributions to put $500 monthly into a down payment fund.

Whatever amount you decide you want to save, have the appropriate amount automatically moved directly out of your bank account with each paycheck on the day the paycheck comes. You can set this up through the brokerage firm or bank you're saving with, or through human resources at work if contributing to a 401(k).

Chapter 7

In and Out

Not all pizza delivery drivers drive fast and

crazy, but there are pressures that encourage it.

    Many drivers are young and inexperienced and those are the drivers that tend to drive faster and more erratic than more experienced drivers.

Drivers are paid like waiters, so most of their income is from tips. Their paycheck mostly pays for taxes and car repairs. The faster the driver gets to a delivery, the higher the tip and the more runs he can take. Basically, the faster they are, the more money they make.

Great work hero the in and out principle of delivery should not be taken with a grain of salt. From the moment you come in to work to the time you leave you should be 100% focused on improving your financial life. You have already created your steps now its time to push hard as delivery drivers we live off the tips and if you don't know it yet no matter what you do there will be a time you are on a roll and then the next customer you approach writes a big fat zero on the tips line for reasons we don't understand or care to understand.

Whatever the case accept the receipt back from customer and say "have a nice day" I see to many delivery drivers get so flustered over this and I just shake my head because if you think about it "There's absolutely nothing you can do about that customer giving you that tip if they are dead set on writing a zero" I have been there it sucks but I'm not going to let that stop me I have a goal to be "wealthy" and I'm going to do everything in my power to achieve that and so can you I believe in you. Cut your losses and move! Every second you spend dreading over a no tip is one second longer you take to grab your next tip its just the name of the game.

When you're in store get your mind right and limit the distraction of your other co-workers its ok to chat and communicate with them when things are not as busy so by no means talk with your friends but keep your focus on the big picture.

In my place of business because of how busy we get at times there is a buzzer that will make a noise by the employee preparing the order to notify the delivery driver that the order is ready to go. Through a designated system the next available driver will take it if that's you or you know that's you coming up prepare yourself and when they ring it or call it out it would be wise to be within a one arms distance. If your store does not have a buzzer or an audible notification device, I would bring it up to the store manager. It's a bit different when it comes to Uber eats, Door Dash, or GrubHub. Your mobile phone is how you receive all notifications and allows you to use your GPS to get to your customers faster. You make MORE money with scheduled blocks, although you can still get earnings without them.

Consequently, if you drop a block or decline a delivery, that will affect your Program Level AND your pay! I highly recommend you know where the hot spots are located and have a physical map (Atlas) old school but it works have it in your vehicle incase things go south on your phone. In the military I was taught it's good to use electronics but know the basics skills in the event it fails.

Chapter 8

Define your Wealth

There is a strong correlation between wealth and happiness, the authors say: "Rich people and nations are happier than their poor counterparts; don't let anyone tell you differently." But they note that money's impact on happiness isn't as large as you might think. If you have clothes to wear, food to eat, and a roof over your head, increased disposable income has just a small influence on your sense of well-being.

To put it another way, if you're living below the poverty line ($22,050 annual income for a family of four in

2009), an extra $5,000 a year can make a huge difference in your happiness. On the other hand, if your family earns $70,000 a year, $5,000 may be a welcome bonus, but it won't radically change your life.

So, yes, money can buy some happiness, but as you'll see, it's just one piece of the puzzle. And there's a real danger that increased income can actually make you miserable—if your desire to spend grows with it. But that's not to say you have to live like a monk. The key is finding a balance between having too little and having too much—and that's no easy task.

American culture is consumption-driven.

The media teaches you to want the clothes and cars you see on TV and the watches and jewelry you see in magazine ads. Yet studies show that people who are materialistic tend to be less happy than those who aren't. In other words, if you want to be content, you should own—and want—less Stuff.

In their personal-finance classic Your Money or Your Life (Penguin, 2008), Joe Dominguez and Vicki Robin argue that the relationship between spending and happiness is non-linear, meaning every dollar you spend brings you a little less happiness than the one before it.

More spending does lead to more fulfillment—up to a

point. But spending too much can actually have a negative impact on your quality of life. The authors suggest that personal fulfillment—that is, being content with your life—can be graphed on a curve that flows in this order

Survival. In this part of the curve, a little money brings a large gain in happiness. If you have nothing, buying things really does contribute to your well-being. You're much happier when your basic needs—food, clothing, and shelter—are provided for than when they're not.

Comforts. After the basics are taken care of, you begin to spend on comforts: a chair to sit in, a pillow to sleep on, a second pair of pants. These purchases, too, bring increased fulfillment. They make you happy, but not as happy as the items that satisfied your survival needs. This part of the curve is still positive, but not as steep as the first section.

Luxuries. Eventually your spending extends from comforts to outright luxuries. You move from a small apartment to a home in the suburbs, say, and you have an entire wardrobe of clothing. You drink hot chocolate on winter evenings, sit on a new sofa, and have a library of DVDs. These things are more than comforts—they're luxuries, and they make you happy. They push you to the peak of the Fulfillment Curve.

Overconsumption. Beyond the peak, Stuff starts to take control of your life. Buying a sofa made you happy, so you buy recliners to match. Your DVD collection grows from 20 titles to 200, and you drink expensive hot chocolate made from Peruvian cocoa beans. Soon your house is so full of Stuff that you have to buy a bigger home—and rent a storage unit. But none of this makes you any happier. In fact, all of your things become a burden. Rather than adding to your fulfillment, buying new Stuff actually detracts from it.

The sweet spot on the Fulfillment Curve is in the Luxuries section, where money gives you the most happiness:

You've provided for your survival needs, you have some creature comforts, and you even have a few luxuries. Life is grand. Your spending and your happiness are perfectly balanced. You have Enough.

Unfortunately, in real life you don't have handy visual aids to show the relationship between your spending and your happiness; you must figure out what enough is on your own. But as you'll see in the next section, because we've been conditioned to believe that more money brings more happiness, most people reach the peak of the Fulfillment Curve and then keep on spending.

Caught Up in the Rat Race typically, as

your income increases, your lifestyle grows with it. When your boss gives you a raise, you want to reward yourself (you deserve it!), so you spend more. All that new Stuff costs money to buy, store, and maintain. Gradually, your lifestyle becomes more expensive so you have to work harder to earn more. You think that if only you got another raise, then you'd have Enough. But in all likelihood, you'd just repeat the process by spending even more.

Psychologists call this vicious cycle the hedonic treadmill, though you probably know it as the "rat race." People on the hedonic treadmill think they'd be happy if they just had a little more money. But when they get more money, they discover something else they want. Because they're never content with what they have, they can never have Enough.

Most Americans are stuck on this treadmill. According to the U.S.

Census Bureau (http://tinyurl.com/census-inc), in 1967 the median American household income was $38,771 (adjusted for inflation). Back then, less than one-fifth of U.S. families had color TVs and only one in 25 had cable. Compare that with 2007, when the median household income was $50,233 and nearly everyone had a widescreen color TV and cable. Americans now own twice as many cars as they did in 1967, and we have computers, iPods, and cellphones. Life is good, right? But despite our increased incomes and material wealth, we're no happier than were in the '60s.

If you don't know why you're earning and

spending money, then you can't say when you have Enough. So take time to really think about what having Enough means to you. Discuss it with your family, and explore the idea with your best friend. Is being debt-free Enough? Being able to pay cash for a new boat? Having a million dollars saved for retirement? Decide what Enough means to you, and then write it down. If you don't have an end in sight, you're at greater risk of getting stuck in the rat race.

Because the notion of Enough is so vague, the best way to approach it is to be mindful of your financial habits. The act of consciously choosing how you spend can help you make purchases that are in line with your goals and values.

Ramit Sethi popularized the concept of conscious spending in his book I Will Teach You to Be Rich (Workman

Publishing, 2009). The idea is to spend with intent, deliberately deciding where to direct your money instead of spending impulsively. Sethi argues that it's okay to spend $5,000 a year on shoes—if that spending is aligned with your goals and values and you've made a conscious choice to spend this way (as opposed to spending compulsively—see Curbing Compulsive Spending).

If you're new to conscious spending, try asking yourself the following questions:

Did I receive value from this equal to the amount I spent? In other words, did you get your money's worth? You already know that $100 spent on one thing isn't always as good as $100 spent on another. Conscious spending is about striving to get the most bang for your buck.

Is this spending aligned with my goals

and values? Conscious spending means prioritizing putting your money toward the things you love—and cutting costs mercilessly on the things you don't. If you're happy with the coffee at the office, then don't waste your money at Starbucks. But if your extra-hot nonfat caramel latte is the highlight of your day, then buy the latte! Spend only on the things that matter to you.

If vast riches won't bring you peace of mind, what will?

In a 2005 issue of the Review of General Psychology, Sonja Lyubomirsky, Kennon Sheldon, and David Schkade looked at years of research to figure out what contributes to "chronic happiness" (as opposed to temporary happiness). Based on their survey, they came up with a three-part model:

About half of your happiness is biological.

Each person seems to have a happiness "set point," which accounts for roughly 50% of your sense of well-being. Because this set point is genetic, it's hard to change.

Another 10% of happiness is based on

circumstances—external factors beyond your control. These include biological traits like age, race, nationality, and gender, as well as things like marital status, occupational status, job security, and income. Your financial situation is part of this 10%—but only a part—which means it accounts for just a fraction of your total happiness.

The final 40% of happiness comes from intentional activity—the things you choose to do. Whereas circumstances happen to you, intentional activity happens when you act by doing things like exercising, pursuing meaningful goals, or keeping a gratitude journal.

According to the authors, because circumstances—including your financial situation—play such a small role in your general contentment, it makes more sense to boost your bliss through intentional activity, by controlling the things you can and ignoring those you can't.

(You can read the entire article at http://tinyurl.com/hmodel.)

Although your financial situation plays

only a small role in your overall happiness, most people believe it's more important than that. Because of this, many Americans spend their lives striving for more money and possessions—but find that this materialism makes them less happy.

If you're caught up in the rat race, you may be dealing with things like credit card debt, living paycheck to paycheck, fighting with your spouse over money, and working a job you hate. These problems all stem from one issue: lack of control. When you feel like you have no control over money, you're worried and stressed. By taking charge of your finances, you can get rid of many of these stressors and be happier. Wealth gives you options and makes it easier to focus on things that can make you content.

Prioritize. Spend on the things that make you happiest. There's nothing wrong with buying things you'll use and enjoy—that's the purpose of money. If you're spending less than you earn, meeting your needs, and saving for the future, you can afford things that make life easier and more enjoyable. (For another way to prioritize, see the box on Living a Rich Life.)

Stay healthy. There's a strong tie between health and happiness. Anyone who's experienced a prolonged injury or illness knows just how emotionally—and financially—devastating it can be. Eat right, exercise, and get enough sleep (*Your Body: The Missing Manual* has loads of tips on how to do all those things).

Don't compare yourself to others. Financially, psychologically, and socially, keeping up with the Joneses is a trap. You'll always have friends who are wealthier and more successful in their careers than you. Focus on your own life and goals.

Limit media exposure. Mass media—especially TV—tries to persuade you that happiness depends on things you don't really need and can't afford. Studies have found that watching lots of TV can influence your levels of materialism—how much you think you need to be happy.

Simplify. The average Joe believes that materialism is the

path to happiness—but the average Joe is wrong. Research shows that materialism actually leads to unhappiness and dissatisfaction. By simplifying your life and reducing the amount of Stuff you own (or want to own), you'll save money and be happier.

    Help others. Altruism is one of the best ways to boost your happiness. It may seem counter-intuitive (and maybe even a little self-serving), but donating to your church or favorite charity is a proven method for brightening your day.

Embrace routine. Emerson wrote, "A foolish consistency is the hobgoblin of little minds," but there's evidence that some consistency is conducive to contentment. In Happier (McGraw-Hill, 2007), Tal Ben-Shahar recommends building routines around the things you love: reading, walking, gaming, knitting, whatever. Because it can be difficult to make the time for these activities, he argues that we should make rituals out of them. If you enjoy biking, make a ritual out of riding to the park every evening, for example. (See the box below for tips on finding time for what you love.)

Pursue meaningful goals. As you'll learn in the next chapter, the road to wealth is paved with goals, and the same is true of the road to happiness. But for a goal to be worthwhile, it has to be related to your values and interests—it has to add something to your life. Chapter 2 will help you decide what goals to set.

The bottom line is that if you can't be content, you'll never lead a rich life, no matter how much money you have. The key to money management—and happiness—is being satisfied. It's not how much you have that makes you happy or unhappy, but how much you want. If you want less, you'll be happy with less. This isn't a psychological game or New Age mumbo-jumbo, it's fact: The lower your expectations, the easier they are to fulfill—and the happier you'll be.

When I think of Wealth the first thing that pops into my head to some of the readers surprise is not money but the ability to do the things that I want in my life without having to stress over the fact on how I'm going to be able to afford this or that. Please do not get Wealth mixed up with just being about the money but view it as a tool to have the freedom to spend the already short amount of time we have on this earth with the people we genuinely care about. Don't get me wrong we work are asses off every day to get paid and have fun when we spend it on the things that matter to us and by no means am I telling you to be frugal and drink out of the public library's fountain just be conscious of your spending and live the Wealthy life you deserve carry this book with you if you find yourself in a rut out there on the road stay humble drivers go out there and get those tips.

ACKNOWLEDGMENTS

I could not have put this book together without the help of my friends who I had the pleasure serving with during the War in Iraq and Afghanistan a very special breed, and to my Domino's crew that continues today to fight through the long hours and rainy days 364 days a year thanks for all you do!

Readers

Thank You!

I deeply appreciate the support you have given me in purchasing this book I spent a great deal of time and sacrificed hours of work to make this happen and I hope this serves you well into the future.

<u>Biography</u>

My name is Jack Robert Masden I was born in the town of Oak Harbor Washington on June 13, 1988. I graduated high school in the year of 2006 and two months later I joined the Marine Corps to serve my country honorably (12 years). I have a loving wife by the name of Martha and a Son that has a heart of gold. I currently work at the Dominos on Camp Lejeune North Carolina.

I like to spend my off time Writing, Exercising and enjoying every moment I can with the family.

Citations

The Mental Health Benefits Of Having A Daily Routine

https://www.blurtitout.org/2018/11/08/menta

l-health-benefits-routine/

13 Habits of Humble People

https://www.forbes.com/sites/jeffboss/2015/03/01/13-habits-of-humble-people/#4e38e17849d5

https://blog.rescuetime.com/growth-mindset-future-of-work/

What Type Of Vehicle Is Best For Delivery Drivers?

https://ridesharecentral.com/vehicle-type-delivery-drivers

The Complete Guide to Automating Your Finances

https://www.doughroller.net/personal-finance/the-complete-guide-to-automating-your-finances/

The Essential Gear for Every Delivery Driver https://www.courierhacker.com/2018/05/23/courier-drivers-gears/

www.ingramcontent.com/pod-product-compliance
Lightning Source LLC
Chambersburg PA
CBHW021813170526
45157CB00007B/2568